Growing flowers

Written by
Tapasi De

Illustrated by
Suman S. Roy

Mum says that trees are our best friends. They always help us.

Trees make our surroundings green and fresh.

One day I told mum that I wanted to plant a tree.

Mum was happy to hear this. She asked me where I wanted to plant it.

I said our garden would be the best place. Mum said that it was a good idea.

She asked me which tree I would like to plant in our garden.

I thought and thought but could not decide.

Mum asked me what I would like to plant—a big tree or a small plant which would give flowers.

This helped me to decide. I said that I would like to plant tulips!

Mum was happy that I had decided what to plant.

In the weekend, she bought tulip bulbs from a nearby nursery.

On Sunday, mum and I went to our garden with the tulip bulbs.

The tulip bulbs looked like small onions with pointed heads.

They were light brown.

We took a shovel, fertilizers and a watering can with water to the garden.

At first we looked for a place where I could plant my buds.

As tulips love sunlight, we looked for a sunny place. At last we found one.

Mum told me to dig the soil and make it loose.

I dug a hole with a shovel. The ground was solid. I had to dig hard.

I dug and dug until the hole was quite big. Mum told me to plant the bulbs into it.

I planted three bulbs into the hole. Then I covered the bulbs with soil so that birds would not eat them.

I had mixed the fertilizer with the soil before covering the seeds with it.

Then I watered the bulbs. The ground became a tiny pool.

I carried the shovel and the watering can inside. Then I washed the mud from my hands.

Though I was a little tired, I was happy.

I told Mum that I could not wait to see my tulips grow. One day, young plants grew from the bulbs that I had planted.

A few days later, tulip buds came out too. I wanted the flowers to bloom at once.

One fine day they did!
They were nodding their
heads in the breeze.

I called dad, mum and my little sister to show them my tulips.

They were all very happy and praised my hard work!

Let's spell new words

surroundings

idea

tulips

garden

thought

decided

pointed

bulb

nursery

fertilizer

watering can

shovel

gap

bloom

dig

nodding

covering

praised